CATHERINE BRIGHTON is a much-exhibited illustrator whose shows
have included Quentin Blake's travelling exhibition *Box of Delights*;
Pictures: English Children's Illustrators in Bologna; and the American Society of Illustrators
Annual Exhibition in New York. She studied at St Martin's School of Art
and the Royal College of Art. Her childhood biographies include *Five Secrets in a Box*,
the story of Galileo's daughter, Virginia; and *Nijinsky*, the early life of
the Russian ballet dancer. *Mozart,* her first book for Frances Lincoln,
was described by *The Junior Bookshelf* as "a volume of real enchantment".
Catherine lives in London.

CHARLOTTE   BRANWELL

EMILY   ANNE

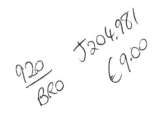

First published in Great Britain in 1994 by
Frances Lincoln Children's Books,
4 Torriano Mews, Torriano Avenue
London NW5 2RZ

www.franceslincoln.com

This edition published in 2004

Distributed in the USA by Publishers Group West

British Library Cataloguing in Publication Data
available on request

ISBN 1-84507-334-7

Printed in China

9 8 7 6 5 4 3 2 1

The BRONTËS

Scenes from the childhood of Charlotte,
Branwell, Emily and Anne

Catherine Brighton

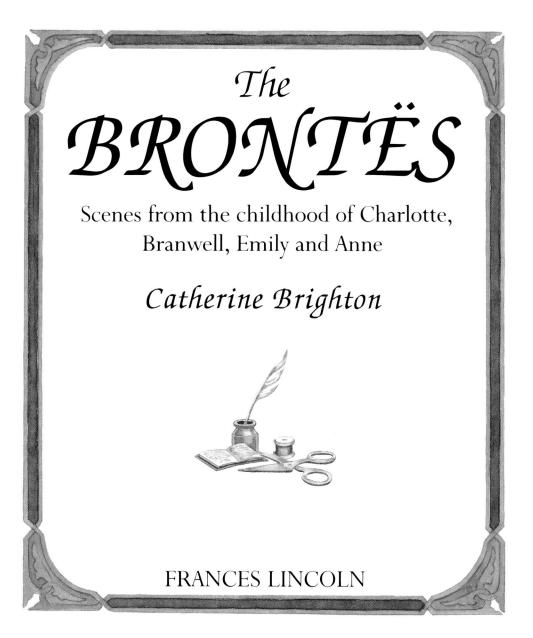

FRANCES LINCOLN

J204,981
£9.00   920
BRO

Prologue

This book is about four extraordinary children: Charlotte, Branwell, Emily and Anne Brontë.

They lived over a hundred years ago in the north of England. Their home was a lonely parsonage by a church in the remote village of Haworth. They never mixed with the village children but played make-believe together in and around the parsonage. When they were very young their mother died, and soon afterwards their two elder sisters, Maria and Elizabeth, died too. Their father, Patrick Brontë, who was the parson of Haworth, invited Aunt Branwell to come and live with them.

Charlotte describes their life together. . . .

The Moors

On Mondays, Tabby the maid scrubs the flagstones and we are forbidden to enter until they are clean and dry.

Papa hurries us into our coats and hats and we follow him happily out on to the moors. Haworth moors are the biggest and best back garden in the world. Emily is carrying her hawk on her gauntlet and the dog runs on ahead.

It is Papa's time for teaching us about God. He waves his arms wide to show God's generosity.

We examine lepidoptera and the calices of flowers with a spy glass, and we study geography and astronomy using Papa's telescope. On our way home we sing hymns as loud as we can. God surely must hear our voices echoing through the darkening hills.

The Great Bogburst

It is September and we are exploring a gully.

Suddenly a storm breaks above us. Lightning fires its arrows into the ground and the rain comes down so hard that rivers and rocks tumble down the steep hillside. The ground opens before our feet and explosions of mud and rocks shoot up in the air.

"It's wonderful!" shouts Emily from a high rock. "It's an earthquake."

At home, dear Papa cannot work. He stands at the lighted window, anxiously waiting and praying for our safe return.

Later, when we are huddled safely around the fire, Aunt Branwell wraps us in blankets. "Truly," I say to Papa, "it was exciting to see the world like it is in the Bible pictures."

The Forbidden Games

Papa has gone to Leeds, and while he is away we play noisy forbidden games. We slide down the bannisters, shout as much as we can and let Emily's geese into the house. We climb Papa's double cherry tree and as dusk creeps over Haworth we play bed plays in the cellar.

We call them bed plays because they are secret.

Sometimes bed plays are about torture. Emily keeps the key and we take it in turns to be the torturer. Branwell is the worst torturer and usually one of us ends up in tears.

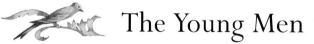 The Young Men

The morning after Papa's return from Leeds, Branwell comes to our bedroom door. He is clutching a red wooden box.

"Look what Papa has brought me. Soldiers!"

"Let's see," I cry. Branwell opens the box and I snatch up a soldier.

"This one shall be mine!" I cry. Emily and Anne do the same.

    We sit holding our soldiers like precious statues until Branwell says, "Let's play battles!"

    So we do, and we call our soldiers the Young Men.

The Battles

Since the Young Men have arrived, our play has become far more exciting. Branwell invents famous battle games and our soldiers are all generals.

Mine is the Duke of Wellington, Emily's is called Gravey because he looks serious and grave, Anne calls hers Waiting Boy (I don't know why) and Branwell has Napoleon Bonaparte so he can have good battles with me.

Sometimes our battles last all day and everyone is dead by the evening. We have invented a rule called *making alive* so the game can continue the next day.

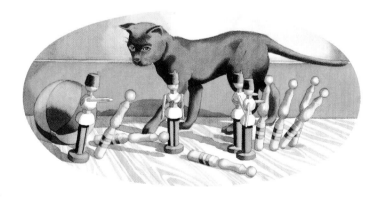

❧❧❧ The Imagination

Sometimes we leave the soldiers in their box. Instead, we make up a whole new city, the Great Glass Town Confederacy. We, the Four Genii, are its rulers and generals.

At night I stand at the window going over in my mind what the Duke of Wellington will do tomorrow. The moon enlightens me.

At dawn the Duke wakes me and I tiptoe to Papa's study. Always I find the answers to my problems in books and atlases. I find the name of a new exotic country, the Duke and I change into explorers and we set sail for new shores.

The Meeting of the Waters

Often we take our made-up characters to our favourite place on the moors called the Meeting of the Waters. If we go for the whole day we pretend that our belongings are the generals' luggage.

Emily, of course, is carrying her hawk, Anne looks after the dog and Branwell has the Young Men in their box. We carry between us a lunch basket, fishing nets and our books. In the heat of summer it feels like foreign travel.

Out of the hazy blue comes a hot air balloon. It silently traverses the sky and I climb in with the Duke. An adventure follows and we are back before Emily has unpacked lunch. What bliss.

The Mask

On Sunday evening Papa calls us to his study and we sit in a line on the sofa.

His voice is droning on as he reads the Holy Bible. My mind returns to the Duke of Wellington, who is in danger. I must save him.

"Charlotte! What must you do to be saved?" Papa is asking me. I have forgotten. I must save the Duke.

Then Papa, seeing we are bored, takes down the mask he keeps on

the wall. He hands it to me and I put it on. When we are wearing it we must tell the truth.

"Where were you just now, Charlotte?" asks Papa. "Something tells me you were elsewhere."

"Yes Papa. I was in Togoland with the Duke of Wellington."

Papa peers at me over his spectacles, takes the mask and returns with a sigh to reading from the Holy Bible.

✂ The Books

We, the Genii, have started to write books. The plays and wild games are going to be written down!

We collect old envelopes and grocery bags and cut the paper into tiny sheets. The covers are made from blue sugar bags and we sew the sides with a needle and thread.

Sometimes we cut and write, read and write, sew and write all morning, all afternoon and until the candles gutter deep into the evening.

Our writing is so tiny, and our books so very small, you can only read them with a magnifying glass.

 ## The Dream

One winter evening Emily plays the piano, while Branwell and Anne read or write their little books. The dog is blinking at the flames.

I sit atop Papa's ladder and look out of the window to where the moors are blanketed in snow.

When the snow stops falling, I can see Glass Town emerging in my mind. I see the Duke of Wellington pass by on his horse and the moon moves in and out of the clouds.

I think that one day I would like to become a famous writer.

Epilogue

The Four Genii continued to write and produce hundreds of little books. Their reading, writing, games and imaginings turned first into poetry and later on, as the girls grew older, into novels.

Charlotte's best-known book is *Jane Eyre*, Emily's is *Wuthering Heights* and Anne's *The Tenant of Wildfell Hall*. Their books have played an important part in the history of English literature.

Branwell tried unsuccessfully to become a writer and painter.

Sadly, they all died when they were still quite young, but they live on through their books.

CHARLOTTE   BRANWELL

EMILY   ANNE

MORE TITLES AVAILABLE IN PAPERBACK
FROM FRANCES LINCOLN

MOZART
Catherine Brighton

When the great composer Mozart was a child he was known as
the 'miracle boy'. Accompanied by his parents and his older sister
Nannerl, he travelled to perform concerts in the grandest palaces in Europe.
Seen through the eyes of Nannerl, this is an enchanting story of achievement,
excitement and very hard work, meticulously researched and brought
to life by Catherine Brighton.

EDISON'S FANTASTIC PHONOGRAPH
Diana Kimpton
Illustrated by M.P. Robertson

Dot's father is working on an invention to read Dot her bedtime story.
But little does she know, the invention will go on to change the world.
Discover the fascinating story of the first recording of sound,
seen through the eyes of Thomas Edison's daughter.

SEVEN WONDERS OF THE ANCIENT WORLD
Mary Hoffman
Illustrated by M.P. Robertson

Philip and his master, the Royal Librarian Callimachus, go on
a marvellous Mediterranean journey, taking in the sights of the
Wonders of the Ancient World. And when they sail home to Alexandria,
there is one more surprise to come.

Frances Lincoln titles are available from all good bookshops.
You can also buy books and find out more about your favourite titles,
authors and illustrators on our website: www.franceslincoln.com